POT-POURRI MAKING

Pot-pourri Making

Illustrated by
Sanmarie Harms

STACKPOLE
BOOKS

© Margaret Roberts 1986

Published by
STACKPOLE BOOKS
5067 Ritter Road
Mechanicsburg, PA 17055

Printed in Hong Kong

10 9 8 7 6 5 4 3 2 1

Originally published by Lowry Publishers in 1986.
Reprinted 1989, 1990, 1992 by David Bateman Ltd.
Cover design by Tracy Patterson with Mark Olszewski.

To the best of their knowledge, the publishers believe that the recipes and information in this book are accurate and will give good results. But recipes and other information cannot take into account the particular circumstances of individual readers, including allergies, sensitivities, and variations in plant material. Readers are advised to consult with physicians on any health or medical condition. Furthermore, information can become out of date and author's or printer's errors can creep in. The publishers cannot therefore be legally responsible for the consequences of any error or omission.

Library of Congress Cataloging-in-Publication Data

Roberts, Margaret (Margaret Joan)
Pot-pourri making / (Margaret Roberts): illustrated by Sanmarie Harms.
p. cm.
Reprint. Originally published: Lowry Publishers, 1986.
ISBN 0-8117-2590-1
1. Potpourris (Scented floral mixture) I. Title.
TT899.4.R63 1994

745.92--dc20   94-5873
                 CIP

Contents

Foreword

When talking of herbs most people think in terms of fragrance and flavour, and in their minds they link that umbrella word 'pot-pourri' with delicate petals, scents, sachets and pomanders. This is what this little book is all about: pot-pourri and how to make and enjoy it, and live with the glory of summer and spring flowers all year through in your home.

Pot-pourri allows you to have a garden within a city flat, a garden to restore your soul and to let you relive the joy of summertime even in the dark of winter. Through these scented pages I hope that you, too, will become an explorer in the realm of magical fragrance and beauty that comes to us from the plant kingdom.

Fragrance is only a part of the pleasure that a bowl of pot-pourri can give, as is the rich visual delight of the dried petals and leaves. I have often been requested for step-by-step instructions, and time and time again I start my workshops and lectures with pot-pourri making. Almost daily a first-time pot-pourri maker knocks on my door or telephones – this book is for those people.

My thanks go to my editor Alison Lowry for her quiet patience, and to my daughter Gail for her support and interest, and for disentangling my enthusiastic dawn writings to type the manuscript. And to all those people who sniffed and inhaled and encouraged and delighted in every new pot-pourri experiment and mixture I have produced over the years, I bless you.

May your pot-pourris give you as much pleasure as mine give me and may this book change your life into a fragrant delight.

1

What is Pot-pourri?

3

According to the dictionary, pot-pourri is a mixture of dried petals and leaves, spices and oils, mixed for fragrance and stored in jars. Literally translated, 'pot-pourri' is French for 'rotten pot' and indeed with some of the recipes you will see why this is so! Some pot-pourris combine moist petals, spices and salt and these are left to rot or ferment; they may end up looking unpleasant but they do smell divine.

The origin of pot-pourri making in its simplest form goes back into the mists of time. Man has always been drawn to the scent of flowers and leaves and has yearned to preserve their fragrances. He has dried and stored them, blended and pressed them, and experimented with flowers gathered in summer meadows.

The earliest recipes favoured the moist method and included strange ingredients like pieces of scented bark, berries, small cones, fruit pips and roots.

Because of unpleasant odours, not to mention the health hazards of the open sewers and drains of just a few centuries

ago, pot-pourri became a necessary detoxifier and anti-pollutant. Fragrant and antiseptic herbs were grown in almost every cottage garden to combat the stench which came off the streets. Herbs were burned in sick-rooms and on funeral pyres and the well-loved 'tussie-mussie', a posie of sweet-smelling herbs and flowers carried on the body, served both as a deodorant and health protector. The dried tussie-mussie went into the pot-pourri bowl, for the scented flowers were regarded as precious and were used to the full.

The word pot-pourri encompassed a host of wonderful ingredients and different blends of herbs, flowers, spices, leaves, resins, barks, seeds, roots, and peels went into the mixtures to be used as disinfectants, for fragrance, cleansing, as sleep aids and room fresheners. As Gerard in his *Herbal* of 1597 so aptly wrote:

'If odours may worke satisfaction, they are so soveraigne in plants and so comfortable;
that no confection of the apothecaries can equall their virtues.'

It was really during the Tudor Age that pot-pourris were developed, and we are able to glean much from their methods and recipes. They called their collection of sweet-smelling flowers and leaves 'sweet pots for keeping'. Most homes had a 'stillroom' in which the lady of the house prepared and made all sorts of sweet-smelling delights. She dried petals, and blended and mixed air fresheners, bath herbs and pomanders. She sewed sachets and little bags, pillows and moth-repellent cupboard bags. She mixed herbs for the sick-room, herbs for the kitchen, and herbs to keep her pantry fresh. It was a serious business and one which absorbed a lot of time.

Tudor gardens were filled with fragrant flowers, lemon and orange trees were grown in conservatories, precious and well tended. Jasmines and stephanotis had their place there too, and hardier plants and those with aromatic leaves were grown outside.

Basic Ingredients

Traditional pot-pourri recipes require six basic ingredients.

Scented flowers such as roses, honeysuckle, heliotrope, lavender, orange blossom, hyssop, violets, carnations, jasmine, pinks, mignonette, stocks, hyacinths, wallflowers, elder, and bergamot.

Scented leaves such as those of scented geraniums, lemon verbena, lemon balm (melissa), eucalyptus, lavender, bay, myrtle, box, sweet basil, rosemary, thyme, sage, mint varieties, lemon and orange, southernwood, yarrow, conifer, cypress, and bergamot. Leaves seem to retain their scent longer than flowers, so are essential in pot-pourris.

Spices are valuable ingredients in holding the perfume of a pot-pourri. Many varieties and blends of spices can be found at the supermarket today, although there are several you can grow yourself, such as coriander, dill, caraway, and ginger. Others easily obtainable are allspice, cardamom, cinnamon, cloves, vanilla pods, nutmeg, mace and juniper. All of them are the berries or bark, seeds or fruits of this exotic range of plants. In protected areas, eg in a hot-house, it is possible to grow vanilla vines, but they will have to be pollinated by hand, unless you can find a vanilla moth to do the job!

Fixatives. If the fragrance in a pot-pourri is to last, a fixative is an essential ingredient, as it retards evaporation of the fragrance and blends the ingredients together. Long ago animal fixatives were used, eg civet, musk and ambergris, but today these have been replaced with synthetic ones. Plant fixatives are made from *roots*, eg orris root or vetiver root, *barks and woods*, eg sandalwood and cedarwood raspings, *resins* (myrrh, frankincense, olibanum, gum benzoin, patchouli), *seeds* (vanilla pods, tonquin or tonka beans), and *peels*, *skins* of fruits (lemon, grapefruit, orange, pomelo, mandarin, kumquat).

The fixatives are a constant problem for pot-pourri makers as many are unobtainable, and those that are available are prohibitively expensive, and the suppliers few and far between. Importing ingredients only adds to the already high costs, and I therefore encourage people to make their own fixatives from cheap, readily available ingredients which can be grown in their own gardens. These are (i) the common or garden iris, and (ii) citrus peels. The old-fashioned purple or white iris is the one to cultivate, and the part to use is the rhizome. Cut off the root hairs and leaves, wash the rhizome, scrubbing off the soil, then mince or grate it finely while still fresh and green. Spread the rhizome gratings out on a piece of newspaper and place in the sun to dry. If you need it powdered, crush or grind it after this stage.

Each time you eat an orange, a mandarin or grapefruit, do not throw away the peel. Mince it finely, but do not dry it first as this makes it too difficult to mince properly. Once it is minced, spread it out on newspaper or on trays in the sun, where it usually takes 2–3 days to dry, depending on the weather. In wet cold winters, dry it in the warmer drawer of the oven, turning it every now and then.

All citrus peelings make an excellent fixative, as do the minced or crushed pips and blossoms.

Essential oils are also known as the aromatic oils, or pot-pourri or flower oils. They are distilled, expressed or extracted from the leaves, berries, flowers, roots or barks of plants. As many tons of flowers go into the making of one little bottle of oil, the pure essential oils can prove to be very costly. Although I prefer not to use synthetic products, I do realize that if we don't use synthetic oils in our pot-pourris, the whole enterprise will work out so expensive as not to be worthwhile.

Sometimes it is possible to reach a happy combination of technical oil base and a pure flower extract, a compromise somewhere between the two. Because there is so much interest in pot-pourri making, many gift shops, chemists and craft shops stock the oils and new fragrances are constantly becoming available to cater for even the most unusual tastes. Favourite essences are rose, lavender, jasmine, honeysuckle, violet, carnation, and geranium. More sophisticated ones include sandalwood, musk, patchouli, ylang-ylang, vetiver or khus-khus grass, bergamot, cedarwood, and spicy combinations. Rosemary, peppermint, cloves, eucalyptus, and lemon oils are often only used medicinally, but combined with other oils, these too can give a rich fragrance.

You can experiment, as I have, with combining and blending fragrances but this is a tricky procedure as there is always a predominant note, and unless one has a particularly keen and sensitive nose, the resulting blur of fragrance is really uninspiring. I would advise sticking to one predominant fragrance and you will find it appealing at all times.

All the commercially available oils are of different strengths, which set the price, so it is advisable to buy from reputable chemists or suppliers. Because of their concentration, it is difficult to ascertain their exact fragrance. The only way to do this when buying your oil is to dip the paper strip provided by aromatic oil suppliers into the oil; a tiny drop onto a little strip of blotting paper will do as well. Smell the paper carefully.

These oils have other attractive uses: Not only do they give that lift to pot-pourris but, added to a carrier such as vegetable oil, can be successfully used for massage, baths, shaken into shampoos, or blended with hand creams. Medicinally they can be combined with almond oil as a rub for aching muscles, while a few drops in a bowl of boiling water will make a cleansing inhalation, eucalyptus, rosemary or peppermint oil being the most effective, to clear congestion in the nose or sinuses. They can also be used as a skin steamer to cleanse and unclog the pores of the skin – lavender, rose, or geranium oils are best for this.

An *essence*, as compared to an essential oil, is basically a proportion of essential oil that is added to alcohol, or wine vinegar. The proportion is usually 1-2 tbsp (12,5-25 ml) oil to 1 litre alcohol or wine vinegar, and then shaken extremely well. Because of the high cost of essential oil, with a little effort you can make your own. Proceed as follows:

Select your favourite aromatic herb, eg lavender, lemon verbena, scented geranium, rosemary, khus-khus grass (vetiver), lemon thyme, lemon mint, peppermint, eau-de-Cologne mint, carnation, jasmine, honeysuckle, or red rose (Crimson Glory is by far the most outstanding).

Select a good vegetable oil that is as odourless as possible, eg sunflower, almond, maize, cotton seed.

Collect a basket of herbs, eg geranium leaves. Chop and macerate enough to fill two-thirds of a 1 litre bottle. Add 2 tbsp (25 ml) white wine vinegar and shake into the chopped green herbs, then fill up the bottle with the oil, shaking well so that vinegar and oil are blended. Stand the bottle in the sun, shaking it daily, for one week. Strain into a kitchen sieve lined with butter muslin or gauze and press out the oil. Add fresh chopped herbs or flowers to the bottle, 2 tbsp (25 ml) white wine vinegar, and shake well. Fill up with oil, shake well again, place in the sun for another week, shaking well daily, and repeat as many times as you feel necessary – usually 4-6 times – until the oil is richly scented. This will give you an abundance of aromatic oil that can be stored indefinitely.

Strain out your final leaves and pour the oil into clean bottles. Store in a cool, dark cupboard. (I store my oil in dark glass bottles as at this stage light dissipates the fragrance.)

Salt is an ingredient often considered unimportant, but to my mind it is essential. In particularly dry climates, pot-pourri is often dry and brittle, and because of this loses a lot of its fragrance. The salt absorbs moisture from the air and in so doing keeps the pot-pourri from drying out and, therefore, retains the scent.

(Salt is a particularly important ingredient in making moist pot-pourris, which are made differently from dry pot-pourris, and these will be discussed fully later in the book.)

The type of salt to use is the unrefined, coarse salt, or rock salt, and not the fine kitchen salt that is refined and iodized. Most supermarkets stock small packages of coarse salt, and butchers, grocers and country stores usually sell bags of it fairly cheaply, as it is the sort fed to cattle. Bay salt, sometimes mentioned in pot-pourri recipes, is sea salt, i.e. salt collected from the bay.

Dry Pot-pourri

The lovely thing about dry pot-pourri making is that it can be a seasonal hobby. You can take your time choosing and collecting your ingredients, and at the same time plan and dream up unusual combinations.

Fragrance is tremendously important in our daily lives, and although today we have sophisticated plumbing and garbage disposal, we now have to contend with industrial pollution. The only satisfying way of doing so, to my mind, is through the natural fragrances of our green heritage.

And what a wealth of fragrant flowers we have at our disposal in our gardens, ranging from glorious, colourful geraniums through to the very exotic tuberoses and citrus trees. A simple combination of only one or two of these beauties makes a delectable pot-pourri.

The drying of petals, flowers and leaves

Many manuals advise you to pick at certain times of the day only and, while it is better to pick in the early morning before the heat of the day has dissipated the oils, in my experience I have picked lavender and geraniums in the late afternoon as well as in the early hours and found no difference in the fragrance and quality of the leaves.

Strong light and heat are not good for either aroma or colour and drying in direct sunlight will result in faded colours. The ideal way to dry is to spread newspapers on a shelf or table in a garage or garden shed. Spread the petals or leaves evenly and not too thickly on the paper and leave for two days. On the third day turn and rearrange them so that all sides dry evenly, and then every day thereafter turn and rearrange them until they are quite dry, stirring and separating each one.

Large shallow trays lined with paper are also excellent, and if you are doing a large amount stretch some shade cloth or butter muslin over a frame and use this. Placing spacers between the frames, you can stack a huge quantity, leaving each tray with enough air circulating around it to allow the flowers to dry evenly.

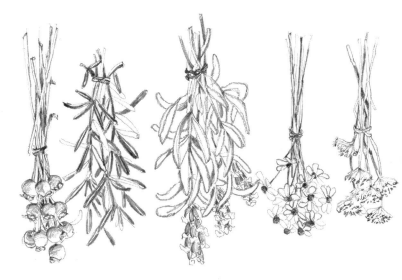

Bunches of herbs can be tied loosely and hung from the ceiling or rafters. Bunches of lavender, sweet basil, larkspur, delphinium, southernwood, and tansy dry beautifully this way.

It is not essential to stick to perfumed blooms only. Many flowers can be added to your pot-pourri for their colour without having a significant fragrance. For example, larkspur, cornflower, delphinium, petrea, daffodils, hibiscus, and peach blossom will do much to enhance a bowl with their rich colours.

In our hot summers I find it takes between 2 and 6 days to dry the leaves and flowers properly. Once dried, pack your first ingredients into brown paper bags and tie the necks of the bags tightly. This keeps them completely fresh and dust free while you dry your other ingredients, such as minced citrus peel, iris roots, bits of bark or seeds.

Dry these as you do the flowers and leaves, spreading them on newspaper. It is best to place iris root and citrus peels in full sun as they tend to get mouldy. Stir often to allow even drying and within two days these too will dry. Berries, bark and seeds sometimes take a little longer.

Patience is the secret with the drying stage. Just one ingredient containing moisture will make your pot-pourri mouldy and damp.

An easy way of drying twiggy herbs such as sprays of marjoram and thyme is to put them into one of those fishnet bags that oranges are sold in. This can then be suspended, and is a space saver if your flat surfaces are already covered in drying herbs and flowers.

There is only one leaf that I know of which does not need to be dried completely before being added to dry pot-pourris, and that is lemon verbena. It is one of the strongest smelling of all herbs and it retains its beautiful fragrance for many years. It is also the only herb that can be picked and immediately tucked into the linen cupboard, with no fear of it causing mildew or mould. It will also keep moths out of your cupboards. Used as a cut flower, it will scent a room and act as a fly repellent.

Equipment for pot-pourri making

Now that you have your collection of petals, leaves and seeds, you will need a few containers for mixing and storing. You probably already have what you need in your kitchen, but if you intend making huge quantities then you will need some substantial utensils.

Ideally, you should have pottery crocks or jars, enamel basins or buckets (unchipped), or wooden kegs or barrels. It is preferable to avoid plastic or asbestos, unless the asbestos has been covered with two to three coats of paint and then lined with sturdy brown paper. Metal can also be used in pot-pourri making. Glass mixing-bowls and wooden spoons, large casseroles with fitting lids, or old-fashioned ginger jars are fine. Keep your eyes open for large crocks or jars, as you will always find them useful.

I have an enormous enamel washing basin in which I mix my pot-pourris, and if you should have an enamel baby's bath, that is even better. Try to find good fitting lids for your storage and maturing bowls and jars.

A pestle and mortar are essential as they are used to grind down the spices and fixatives. A pepper-mill or coffee-mill will do as well to grind down your blended spices quickly and effectively. You will need measuring jugs to help you with your marking of quantities of oils, as well as a kitchen scale, tablespoons, cups, scoops etc. Use an eye-dropper for measuring oils drop by drop; all chemists stock these.

A pair of rubber gloves can be useful if you prefer not to let your hands come into contact with the mixture. Some recipes can make your hands smell fairly strongly for a few days.

General mixing method

One of the secrets of good pot-pourri making is to mix for longer than you think is necessary. The more you mix the more perfect the blend, and the more each petal comes into contact with the spices and fixatives.

This is a basic method on how to make or mix your pot-pourri, giving the simple outlines of an uncomplicated pot-pourri mixture. It is adaptable to any recipe.

Into a large basin place the following: *bone-dry petals* (eg roses, jasmine, carnations), *dried leaves* (eg geranium, lemon verbena, lavender, eucalyptus, herbs, grasses) and *dried seeds* (eg barks, berries).

Mix well, lifting and taking from the inside of the heap out, and bringing the outside of the heap in. Add salt (dry) and mix again. Add spices and mix again. Add fixative and mix again. Lastly, add drops of essential oil. Mix well, and then mix again, stirring and working finely through the heap. Now turn the mixture into a big crock or jar, seal well and allow to stand for one week.

After a week, open the jar, stir and mix, smell it and add more spices or oil as necessary. Seal and allow to stand for another week. This maturing process is very important as it gives the pot-pourri its long-lasting mellowness and beauty.

If at this point you are not happy with the fragrance, add more dried petals and leaves, and reassess your oils, adding a little at a time. Give your pot-pourri six weeks to two months to settle and blend. If it smells wonderful but looks a little dull or colourless, add some dried marigolds or delphiniums, straw flowers or everlastings to pretty it up. Remember that pot-pourri is an ongoing thing and once your basic mixture is ready bits and pieces can be added.

Special occasion flowers, such as those used for weddings, christenings or anniversary arrangements, can be turned into pot-pourri. I have made many just such special pot-pourris for a bride, or for a special occasion. They look particularly beautiful if some of the flowers are pressed to retain their shape and the pot-pourri bottled in a glass jar with the pressed flowers slipped down the sides. It can make a wonderful reminder of a happy occasion. All that is needed to guarantee years of pleasure are a few drops of essential oil of the predominant flower.

Dry Pot-pourri
Recipes

The following is a collection of dry pot-pourri recipes that have become my favourites. Each one is easy to make and the pleasure each will give over the years is enormous compared to the amount of preparation and work involved.

The measures given are approximate, and quantities can be increased or decreased according to your needs or to what you have available. Always feel free to readjust and add other ingredients. Pot-pourri making is rather like painting a picture; it is in the artist's hands to paint an unforgettable picture, or to paint an ordinary one. The way your mixtures turn out is up to you, and these recipes will, I hope, give you inspiration.

Summer Garden Pot-pourri

10 cups dried rose petals
5 cups lavender flowers and leaves
5 cups scented geranium leaves
2 cups lemon verbena leaves
1 cup honeysuckle flowers
1 cup crushed cinnamon and nutmeg, mixed
1 cup salt
3 cups minced, dried orange and lemon peel
1 cup minced iris root (mixed with gum benzoin, if you can get it)
honeysuckle oil or rose oil

Use general mixing method.

Rose Pot-pourri

10 cups dried rose petals of mixed colours
1 cup dried lemon peel mixed with orange and grapefruit peel
1 cup salt
1 tbsp (12,5 ml) rose oil
½-1 cup crushed cloves and coriander seeds

Use general mixing method.

Fresh Green Pot-pourri

Makes a wonderful deodorant as it helps to clear a smoky atmosphere.

5 cups lemon verbena leaves
5 cups scented geranium leaves
5 cups lemon leaves
2 cups eucalyptus leaves
5 cups peppermint leaves
3 cups lemon peel, minced and dried
3 cups salt
½-1 tbsp (6-12,5 ml) geranium oil
½ tbsp (6 ml) peppermint oil

Use general mixing method.

Winter Pot-pourri

This pot-pourri is a fragrant room freshener.

5 cups lavender leaves
5 cups lemon or orange leaves
3 cups southernwood leaves
3 cups eucalyptus seeds and pods
3 cups deodar or pine needles
a few cypress cones
3 cups salt
3 cups rosemary leaves
1 cup cinnamon and nutmeg, crushed
3 cups minced orange, lemon and mandarin peel (dried)
½-1 tbsp (6-12,5 ml) lemon oil
½-1 tbsp (6-12,5 ml) lavender oil

Use general mixing method, then place in an open bowl near the fire. Stir frequently. Close the bowl or pot with a tight-fitting lid when you are not in the room to enjoy it. Revive from time to time with a little lavender oil.

Tropical Summer Pot-pourri

5 cups gardenias
5 cups jasmine
5 cups tuberoses
3 cups orange blossom
5 cups mint leaves
3 cups honeysuckle flowers
1 cup iris root, minced and dried
3 cups lemon peel, minced and dried
1 cup salt
½-1 tbsp (6-12,5 ml) jasmine or neroli oil

Use general mixing method. Note that this recipe has no spices as the iris or orris root is all important. It is heady and exotic, and it is not advisable to use it in the bedroom as it is too strong to sleep with. Revive with jasmine oil from time to time.

Springtime Pot-pourri

An exquisite pot-pourri for the bedroom.

5 cups wisteria flowers
2 cups violets
5 cups mock orange blossom (philadelphus)
2 cups orange blossom
2 cups freezias (the yellow ones give a gorgeous colour)
2 cups narcissus flowers
1 cup iris root, minced
1 cup grapefruit or lemon peel, minced and dried
1 cup salt

Use general mixing method. Add ½-1 tbsp (6-12,5 ml) violet oil. From time to time revive with violet oil, mixed into a little iris or orris root.

Victorian Pot-pourri

5 cups bergamot leaves and flowers
5 cups scented geranium leaves
5 cups lemon verbena leaves and flowers
5 cups lemon thyme leaves
5 cups rose petals
3 cups sage flowers
2 cups orange and lemon peel, minced and dried
½ cup cloves and nutmeg
½ cup coriander, crushed
½-1 tbsp (6-12,5 ml) geranium or rose oil

Use general mixing method. Fill bowls and place throughout the house. Revive with geranium oil from time to time.

Kitchen Pot-pourri

5 cups lemon thyme leaves
5 cups lemon leaves
5 cups lemon balm (melissa) leaves
5 cups mint
5 cups rosemary leaves
5 cups sweet basil
3 cups mixed lemon and grapefruit peel, minced and dried
2 cups salt
½-1 tbsp (6-12,5 ml) rosemary or lemon oil
1 cup mixed cloves, cinnamon and nutmeg

Use general mixing method. Place in bowls or make into sachets and put them into your kitchen cupboards and drawers. Revive with rosemary oil from time to time.

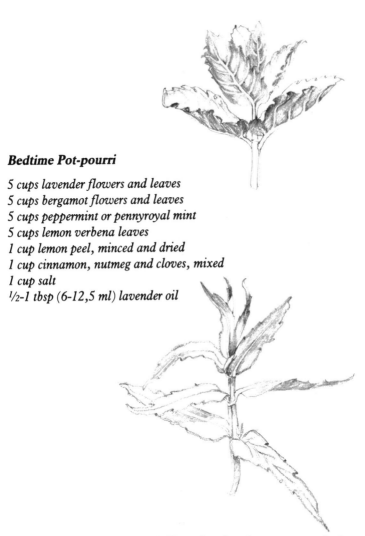

Bedtime Pot-pourri

5 cups lavender flowers and leaves
5 cups bergamot flowers and leaves
5 cups peppermint or pennyroyal mint
5 cups lemon verbena leaves
1 cup lemon peel, minced and dried
1 cup cinnamon, nutmeg and cloves, mixed
1 cup salt
½-1 tbsp (6-12,5 ml) lavender oil

Use general mixing method. Keep in a bowl next to your bed, reviving from time to time with lavender oil. Cover the bowl during the day. This pot-pourri can also be used to stuff pillows and sachets.

Comforting Pot-pourri

This is another bedroom pot-pourri. It will help you to relax.

3 cups eau-de-Cologne mint
5 cups lavender
3 cups rosemary
5 cups geranium leaves
5 cups rose petals
3 cups lemon balm (melissa)
2 cups citrus peel, minced and dried
1 cup salt
1 cup cinnamon and cloves, mixed
½-1 tbsp (6-12,5 ml) rose or geranium oil
a few drops peppermint oil

Use general mixing method. Place in open bowls in the bedroom. Cover when not in the room and revive from time to time with rose oil.

Insect-repelling Pot-pourri

5 cups rosemary
5 cups lavender
3 cups pennyroyal mint
2 cups khakiweed
5 cups southernwood
2 cups yarrow
2 cups citrus peel, minced and dried
1 cup salt
1-1½ cups cloves, coriander and nutmeg, mixed
1 tbsp (12,5 ml) lavender oil

Use general mixing method. This recipe can be used to fill sachets to hang in cupboards. Revive with lavender oil from time to time. Place in bowls in cupboards and behind books and records.

Strong Insect-repelling Pot-pourri

5 cups peppermint or pennyroyal mint
5 cups artemisia absinthium leaves
3 cups khakiweed
3 cups southernwood
3 cups rosemary
3 cups marigold flowers (Tagetes species)
2 cups salt
2 cups orange peel, minced and dried
1 tbsp (12,5 ml) rosemary oil

Use general mixing method. This pot-pourri can be spread loosely behind books and in cupboards, or made up into sachets. Revive from time to time with rosemary oil.

Kitchen Herb Pot-pourri

This pot-pourri has such a beautiful 'herby' fragrance that it is mouth-watering! It freshens up the kitchen wonderfully.

5 cups rosemary
3 cups marjoram
5 cups sage
3 cups peppermint or pennyroyal mint
1 cup salt
1 cup lemon peel, minced and dried
1/2-1 tbsp (6-12,5 ml) lemon oil
1 cup coriander seeds, crushed

Use general mixing method. Stir often to release the fragrance.

Spicy Pot-pourri

This is an unusual pot-pourri. It is very rich and spicy and cannot be left open for too long as it is so strong. I keep it near the fireplace in winter as the warmth draws out the scent and enriches the whole room.

2 cups cinnamon sticks
3 cups cypress leaves, dried
2 cups cypress cones
2 cups eucalyptus seeds
1 cup allspice berries
1 cup nutmeg, crushed
1 cup coriander seeds, crushed
1 cup whole cloves
3 cups myrtle leaves, dried
1 cup myrtle berries, crushed and dried
1 cup salt
1 tbsp (2,5 ml) oil of cloves

The berries, bark and seeds need to be bruised or broken up to allow the scent to escape. Blend and store in a crock for one month without opening, but shake it up daily.

Then spoon out into jars, and you will find it will last for years. Add a few cloves and a little nutmeg (crushed) from time to time, with a few drops of clove oil.

Moist Pot-pourri

Moist pot-pourri differs from a dry mixture in that the petals or flowers and leaves used are not fully dried, and the mixture requires time to mature or blend – and this can sometimes be too long for the impatient! Moist pot-pourri is not very attractive to look at, but its fragrance is rich and mellow and it is so worthwhile that one forgives its appearance.

There are advantages to making moist pot-pourris, one being that the natural aromatic oils in the leaves and flowers are retained for a longer period of time in the moist state. Then the slow maturing and absorption and blending of spices, flower essences, oils, and fixatives give a rich fullness of strength and enduring fragrance that the dry pot-pourris cannot produce. Always keep the containers closed, or their lids firmly on when not in use, and you will find the moist pot-pourri lasts many years, needing only a little attention from time to time.

General mixing method

The general method of moist pot-pourri making is as follows:

Pick a quantity of fragrant flowers (eg rose petals). Immediately spread the petals out on newspapers in the shade and leave overnight to wilt. Next day take a large jar, crock or bucket with a tightly fitting lid and spread a layer of wilted petals over the bottom, about 1" (3 cm) deep. Over this sprinkle a thin layer of coarse salt. On top of the salt sprinkle a few cinnamon chips, crushed cloves and crushed nutmeg. Cover with a layer of rose petals.

Repeat these three layers until your rose petals are used up. Weight down and seal the jar. When you are ready to add more petals, stir the contents well and press down with a good weight (eg a big flat stone). As the summer progresses add more layers of other fragrant flowers, all wilted overnight, alternating with salt and spices. Press down well each time.

As a general guide, to every 6 cups well pressed down petals, add 1 cup salt and ½ cup spices. Any fragrant flowers can be added – orange blossom, violets, honeysuckle, mock orange (philadelphus), sweet peas, scented geraniums. Always remember to stir the previous lot thoroughly before adding new petals and press down well.

As I usually make a substantial quantity, I have an old bread board that fits snugly into my big bucket of petals and I use this to stamp down. If my bucket or bin is not full, I weight the bread board with a stone.

The secret is to keep the petals and salt well pressed together – one could call it 'a pickling of petals'!

Soon frothing and fermentation occur, but do not be alarmed. This is the true 'rotten pot'. Stir your mixture well, and if liquid collects at the bottom and you feel it's too wet, drain it off and let it all stand for 7-10 days.

At this point the fragrance isn't very exciting, but do persist, because soon it will be heady.

As soon as the crock is full and has stood undisturbed for about a week, empty it out onto a big sheet of brown paper or onto a scrubbed tabletop. Break up the conglomerate mass. Now mix in your essential oil. For 10 cups of pot-pourri add approximately ½-1 tbsp (6-12,5 ml) oil. If, for example, you have used predominantly roses, you will add rose oil. At this stage you will want to experiment to suit your individual taste.

Add in more spices (eg crushed coriander, crushed allspice, cinnamon, cloves, nutmeg, etc). For 10 cups pot-pourri, add ½-1 cup mixed spices, depending on your taste. To the above proportions add 1–3 cups minced, dried orange, lemon, mandarin or grapefruit peel – this is a 'fixing' agent.

Mix together well and return the mixture to your original bucket or crock. Cover loosely. Store in an undisturbed place for 6 weeks.

Place your pot-pourri in individual jars and bowls with lids, and set these around the house. Open the bowls for fragrance, close them when you're not in the room. Revive from time to time with a few drops of essential oil and a little spray of water. Stir well.

Once you have grasped the general recipe, experiment on your own, using seasonal flowers. I use my moist pot-pourri as an air freshener in the bathroom and toilet, bedrooms and kitchen and they give off their rich scent for many years. The following are some special recipes which have become favourites of mine through the years.

Moist Pot-pourri Recipes

Clove Air Freshener

Place a bowl in your bathroom and toilet.

10 cups wilted red rose petals
3 cups coarse salt
2 cups whole cloves and cinnamon sticks, crushed and mixed
½ cup (125 ml) oil of cloves

Use general mixing method.

Carnation Moist Pot-pourri

A heady, sweet pot-pourri, best in the living room.

10 cups carnation flowers, pinks, dianthus varieties, broken up,
*   calyx split open*
5 cups jasmine flowers
4 cups coarse salt
1 cup crushed cloves and cinnamon, mixed
¼-1 tbsp (3-12,5 ml) carnation oil
few drops clove oil

Use general mixing method.

Sleep-inducing Bedroom Moist Pot-pourri

5 cups lavender flowers and leaves
5 cups scented geranium flowers and leaves
2 cups peppermint leaves
3-4 cups coarse salt
1 cup allspice, nutmeg and cinnamon,
*   crushed and mixed*
¼ cup (60 ml) lavender oil
few drops peppermint oil

Use general mixing method. After maturing, place in bowls at
the bedside, and stir every now and then. Keep covered in the
day and partially covered at night. The lavender helps one
sleep, the peppermint and geranium have calming properties,
clear sinuses and relieve tension.

Rosemary and Geranium Air Freshener

For the living room, bedroom and bathroom.

5 cups rosemary leaves and flowers
5 cups rose geranium leaves
4 cups coarse salt
2 cups nutmeg, cinnamon, cloves and
*   coriander seeds, crushed and mixed*
½-2 tbsp (6-25 ml) rose geranium oil
few drops rosemary oil

Use general mixing method.

Herb Garden Air Freshener

This is a fresh and invigorating air freshener that is particularly good in the kitchen.

2 cups each mint leaves, sweet basil leaves, rosemary leaves and
*   flowers, sage leaves, lemon verbena leaves*
3 cups coarse salt
1 cup allspice berries, cloves and coriander seeds, mixed and
*   crushed*
½-2 tbsp (6-25 ml) rosemary oil
few drops peppermint oil

When making this pot-pourri add fresh rosemary and lemon verbena leaves. Don't let them wilt as they are a dry type of leaf anyway. Otherwise use the general mixing method. To revive, add a few fresh peppermint and lemon verbena leaves from time to time and a few drops of essential oil. Place in a bowl in the kitchen and stir the mixture frequently.

Springtime Moist Pot-pourri

A beautiful pot-pourri for the bedroom and bathroom.

5 cups narcissus flowers, well pressed down in the cup
2 cups violets
3 cups wisteria flowers
1 cup mock orange (philadelphus) flowers
3-4 cups coarse salt
1 cup cinnamon and nutmeg, mixed and crushed
¼-1 tbsp (3-12,5 ml) violet oil

Use general mixing method.

41

Exotic Moist Pot-pourri

This has a very rich and heady perfume, so use only in the living room.

3 cups orange blossom
2 cups jasmine flowers
2 cups tuberose flowers, broken up
3 cups coarse salt
3 cups gardenias, broken up
1 cup cloves and cinnamon, crushed
¼-1 tbsp (3-12,5 ml) jasmine oil

Use general mixing method.

Cupboard Freshener

I use this pot-pourri in cupboards that store blankets and winter jerseys. It is predominantly lavender and this seems to help combat silverfish. At the start of winter you will find your blankets and winter sheets fresh and fragrant. I also make small sachets of muslin bags and fill them with this pot-pourri to tuck into jerseys and the pockets of winter jackets. It takes away that musty smell, and keeps cupboards beautifully scented. Revive the pot-pourri from time to time with a few drops of lavender oil. Gather the lavender leaves and flowers on a dry day.

10 cups lavender leaves and flowers, well pressed together
3 cups coarse salt
1 cup coriander seeds, crushed
1 cup cinnamon and nutmeg, mixed and crushed
½-1 tbsp (6-12,5 ml) lavender oil

Immediately layer lavender alternately with salt. You will notice that you do not need to dry the lavender partially or wilt it overnight as there is very little moisture in it, and it soon blends and softens in the salt and spices. Pack the jar or crock

well, weight down and leave for 10 days, then break up and mix the rather unattractive mass, and add more spices and the oil. Stand unweighted for another 10 days, then place in jars with loose fitting lids or in sachets in cupboards.

You will notice that in all my recipes I have used rather a large quantity of essential oil. If this makes you nervous, start with a few drops, work the mixture and allow it to stand overnight. Add more oil the following day until the fragrance is pleasing to you.

All the recipes are flexible and are merely given as guidelines for you. There are no hard and fast rules, only basic principles. The weather, too, has some bearing on moist pot-pourri making, as does whether you live at the coast or in the dry mountain air. Experimentation is the only way for the pot-pourri enthusiast to attain satisfaction, and this is what makes pot-pourri making such an absorbing hobby.

Different Uses for Pot-pourri

Now that you have become familiar with pot-pourri making and have started to experiment with some of the more unusual ingredients and recipes, all sorts of ideas of how to use your fragrant delights will present themselves. Filling bowls and jars will simply not be enough, although by now you will probably have quite a collection of pot-pourri containers. Let's explore a little further and find additional uses for our experiments.

Sachets

A sachet is a small perfumed bag that is laid amongst clothes and linen and placed in cupboards and drawers to scent and freshen.

The simplest way of making a sachet is to sew three sides of a square or oblong of muslin, organdy or cotton material, or a material that is thin and finely woven. Choose pretty, soft

colours, perhaps sew on an edging of lace, and fill the sachet with your pot-pourri mixture. Tie with a satin ribbon.

Any pot-pourri recipe is suitable for sachets, but a basic lavender moth-repellent one is probably the most useful and practical. The following is a basic sachet pot-pourri recipe:

Sachet Pot-pourri

5 cups lavender flowers and leaves, mixed
5 cups lemon verbena leaves
3 cups southernwood, tansy, or yarrow, or combinations thereof
1 cup khakiweed
1 cup cloves, roughly crushed
½ cup cinnamon, roughly broken up
2 cups dried lemon peel, minced
1 tbsp (12,5 ml) lavender oil

Use general mixing method. After maturing, fill sachets, and revive from time to time with a few drops of lavender oil. To do this open the sachet and shake the contents out into a plastic bag, add a few crushed cloves, some freshly dried lavender leaves and flowers, and then the oil. Shake well, and leave for 24 hours. Shake up again and refill your washed and ironed sachet. Over the years pot-pourri does need to be revived and added to, but, tended carefully, it can last a lifetime.

Pillow Pot-pourri

Many years ago I developed a 'peace pillow' which is still as popular today as it was then. I never seem to make enough! The pot-pourri with which I fill my pillows is a soothing, calming mixture and the only type of pot-pourri that seems to suit everyone's taste. The lavender in it relieves stress, fatigue and headaches, while the lemon verbena and pennyroyal clear the nose and freshen the sinuses. The rose petals have a calming effect and the combination is altogether most pleasing.

A pillow 30 x 22 cm (9 x 12 inches) seems to be the most practical size as it fits perfectly into the neck and under the head. It is a good idea to use polyester cotton or calico as an inner lining, and make a cover to go over it in a pretty soft fabric, edged with lace or a satin ribbon. Choose a fabric that can be washed frequently so that the pillow can always be dust free and fresh.

The quantities in this recipe fill one peace pillow.

2 cups lavender flowers and leaves
2 cups lemon verbena leaves
2 cups rose petals
½ cup lemon peel, minced and dried
1 cup pennyroyal mint
½ cup cloves and cinnamon, mixed and crushed
1 tsp (5 ml) lavender oil
2-3 drops peppermint oil (if desired)

Use general mixing method. When mature, mix 4-8 cups foam sponge chips into your pot-pourri for added comfort. Stuff the pillow. To revive the fragrance, shake out the pot-pourri mixture every now and then into a large plastic bag. Add a little freshly dried lavender and rose petals, a few pieces of crushed cinnamon and cloves, and a few drops of lavender oil. (I blend the new petals and leaves with the oil first, then add it all to the pillow mixture in order to prevent the foam chips absorbing all the essential oil.)

Shake well, leave for 24 hours, shake again and re-stuff the freshly washed pillow.

Certain herbs are especially kind to the skin and soften the water in one's bath beautifully. Handfuls of loose herbs in the bathwater are not practical, but net or muslin bags filled with herbs, or a mixture tied up in a net square, are ideal.

The two recipes that follow are basic recipes for bath-bags and wash-balls, but here again experimenting with different types of herbs and combinations will give you much pleasure.

Pot-pourri Bath-bags

This quantity fills approximately 12 bags.

4-6 cups rosemary leaves
4-6 cups lavender leaves
2-4 cups yarrow leaves
*2-4 cups mint leaves (peppermint, eau-de-Cologne mint or
    spearmint)*
1 cup dried orange mandarin or grapefruit peel, coarsely chopped
few drops lavender oil

Dry leaves on newspaper in the shade and mix when thoroughly dry. Add chopped peel, then a few drops of lavender oil. Mix well. Leave to stand in a closed container for about a week. Tie into small muslin bags or squares of net. Store in a closed jar until needed. Toss a bag into the bath under the running hot water tap. Rub your soap over the wet bag and use it as a sponge to lather your whole body.

Rinse the bag under the tap after your bath and hang it up to dry. A bag will last for 3 or 4 baths and should then be thrown away.

Suitable bath herbs are rosemary, mint varieties, thuja and conifer varieties, bergamot, scented geranium, sage, chamomile, lemon thyme, elderflowers, yarrow, lavender, and lemon and orange leaves.

Pot-pourri Wash-balls

This quantity fills approximately 12 wash-balls. Tie up in squares of butter muslin or net, or make a little pouch about 10 x 12 cm (4 x 5 inches), sewing up three. sides and tying at the top.

5 cups geranium leaves
3 cups bergamot leaves
3 cups cypress leaves
2 cups good bath soap, coarsely grated
2 cups large oat flakes (not instant oats)
geranium oil

Dry the herbs well and combine with the soap and oats. Add a few drops of geranium oil. Mix well and allow to stand in a closed container for a week. Mix again, and tie into balls, or fill small bags. Use the wash-balls as a soapy sponge, rubbing on more soap where necessary. Use for 3 or 4 baths, drying the bags out between baths, and then throw them away.

Pot-pourri Pastilles

This is an old-fashioned way of making scented beads or pastilles with flowers and spices. They can be placed in drawers where their fragrance will be evident for many years.

Mince a quantity of fragrant rose petals finely, until you have enough to fill 4 cups. To this add ½-1 cup cloves, crushed in a pestle and mortar. Add the following:

½-1 cup crushed cinnamon sticks
1 cup gum benzoin, crushed
½-1 cup glycerine
¼-½ tbsp (3-6 ml) rose oil

Mix ingredients into a thick paste, form into pastilles or marbles by rolling them between your fingers and thumb, pressing well together. Allow to dry thoroughly.

It is not easy to be precise about quantities as success depends on the amount of moisture in the rose petals. It is best to begin with small quantities which can be added to if the texture is not correct so that the mixture does not cohere. If you wish to thread the pastilles, make a hole with a thin knitting needle before they harden.

Pot-pourri Burning Perfume

This is a richly fragrant pot-pourri. It may be heated in a metal dish on a heater or beside the fire. It is not meant to be ignited!

1 cup bergamot leaves and flowers
1 cup lemon verbena
½ cup crushed cloves
½ cup crushed cinnamon
½ cup iris or orris root, minced
few drops oil of clove
few drops oil of honeysuckle

Dry all the herbs well, then combine all ingredients and add as many drops of essential oil as you find pleasing. Shake well and store in a jar for a week, shaking daily. Fill a metal dish from the jar with enough pot-pourri to give a rich fragrance. When not in use return to the jar, add a few drops essential oil and shake well. Keep the jar closed while pot-pourri is not needed.

Herbal Incense

The maturing time for this pot-pourri is several months! The longer it matures the better the result, but when it finally emerges it is so satisfying and unusual you will have to admit it was well worth the trouble.

This recipe is a basic one, lending itself to the inclusion of rarer ingredients such as tonka beans and vetiver root (khus-khus grass). In fact I grow, with ease and great success, an enormous tuft of the latter just for this purpose.

It is the root that holds the perfume and it is amazingly long lasting. Once, when digging up my clump of vetiver to replant and divide it, my little fox-terrier made himself a fragrant bed amongst the dug up and trimmed roots and leaves. He slept there all afternoon while I was busy working in the herb garden and when he came into the house that evening we were stunned by his rich and sophisticated perfume, which lasted all week!

It is not essential to use all of the ingredients in this incense, but substitute where you can to keep it more complete.

½ cup crushed cinnamon
3 tsp (15 ml) rose oil

Optional:

½ cup sandalwood or cedar raspings
½ cup dried lemon peel, minced
½ cup vanilla pod, minced
½ cup crushed tonka beans

Mix well, crushing larger pieces in a pestle and mortar. Place in a sealed jar, shaking daily for at least 2 months. When ready to use, place a small quantity (about 2 tbsp) on a metal dish in a small heap and set alight. If the incense has not fully dried, it will tend to smoulder, so keep pushing lighted matches into it.

Other suitable ingredients, which all need to be well dried and minced or crushed: lemon verbena, lavender leaves, tansy leaves, rosemary leaves, lemon and orange peel, lemon leaves, nutmeg, allspice, angelica root, tonka beans.

Scented Paper

While your pot-pourri is maturing in its closed container, this is an excellent time to make scented paper – writing paper and envelopes, drawer lining paper, blotting or wrapping paper. Simply lay the paper on top of the scented mixture and it will absorb the beautiful fragrance of your pot-pourri.

If you have ever had the pleasure of receiving a letter on scented paper, you will know that it remains in one's heart a long time, and it is such an easy thing for the pot-pourri maker to do. Make sure not to cover the paper with pot-pourri as

there may be little essential oil particles that would mark it with oily patches. Merely lay the paper on top of the petals.

It isn't necessary to restrict yourself to scented paper. Other objects, pine-cones for example, also absorb the fragrance. Bury a cone deep in the pot-pourri once you have placed a few drops of essential oil into each of the cone's little 'petals'. Once you are ready to start using your matured pot-pourri, shake out the pine-cone, tie a pretty ribbon onto it and hang it in a cupboard, in a cloakroom, or even on the Christmas tree. It will give off a beautiful perfume for a long time. It can be revived by plunging it into your next bucket or jar of pot-pourri mixture.

I have used the same method for several different types of seed-pods, for example jacaranda pods, flamboyant seeds, eucalyptus nuts, and liquid amber seeds, and they all work beautifully. Try experimenting with seeds of various types, remembering to paint them first with a little essential oil. An arrangement of treated seeds in a basket placed near the fire in winter makes a fragrant focal point and one that will be a lively conversation piece.

Pomanders

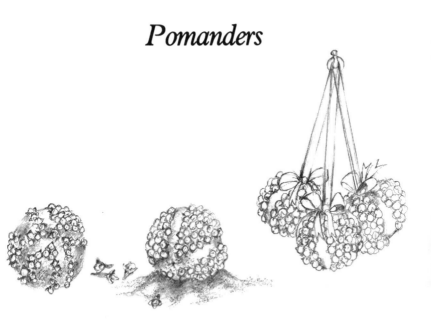

Many centuries ago a pomander was an enviable possession. It belonged invariably to the rich and was used to dispel the bad odours and germs that clogged the city streets. It was mainly worn as an ornament. The French term 'pomme d'ambre', meaning 'apple of ambergris', came to be identified with a small decorative case, usually made from ivory, silver, gold or carved and polished wood, inside which was a small, apple-shaped ball of ambergris (extracted from the sperm whale). The case was attached to a chain and could thus be worn around the neck or waist, or hooked to a watch-chain. Pomanders in fact became ornaments of high fashion.

China and pottery pomanders gradually replaced the expensive and delicately wrought silver and gold cases. They are still popular today and come in a variety of sizes and styles. Basically they consist of a small ball, perforated in order to allow the fragrance to escape. A cork, usually underneath, blocks the opening, and a hanging ribbon is threaded through the top. Filled with a blend of fragrant herbs and spices, these attractive ornaments can be hung in cupboards or from clothes hangers to keep cupboards smelling fresh.

An old-fashioned homemade pomander, using an orange, can be made by anyone and its fragrance lasts for many years. Follow these few simple steps:

Choose a small orange, a good quantity of whole cloves, and a knitting needle. Prick holes in the orange, close together, press the cloves deeply into the holes, and cover the orange completely, rather like a pincushion. Using florist's wire, make a loop by pressing the ends into the orange. This is in order to thread a piece of ribbon through it so that the fruit can be hung up. Meanwhile into a brown paper bag place the following mixture:

¹/₂ cup powdered orris root
¹/₂ cup ground cinnamon
¹/₂ cup ground cloves
few drops clove oil

Place your orange in the bag and shake thoroughly so that it is completely covered by the mixture. Shake every day for about a month, at all times keeping the bag tightly closed. When you finally remove the orange from the bag it will have dried out and shrunk. Shake off the excess spice mixture, thread a ribbon through the loop and hang it in your cupboard.

Several types of citrus fruit are suitable for making pomanders, but I find that it is the smallest possible which work the best. Small lemons, mandarins, kumquats are all worth using. One idea is to make clusters of clove-studded kumquats to hang in the kitchen or pantry on thin gold thread of different lengths – the effect is most striking.

Always choose ripened fruit and always give it one month to mature and dry out. If your orange or lemon is too big and juicy it will become mouldy, so do look out for the small ones.

If ever you feel the need for extra fragrance, just pop your pomander back into a paper bag filled with the orris root and spices. Shake it up for a week or so and add a few drops of essential clove oil from time to time.

Pomander Beads

This is a special recipe of lavender beads that can be threaded into a necklace or rosary (or can be put into a pomander).

1 cup lavender flowers
1/2 cup minced, powdered sweet flag root
1/2 cup gum benzoin
1/2 cup sandalwood raspings, powdered
2 tsp (10 ml) lavender oil
few drops violet oil
2-3 tsp (10-15 ml) gum tragacanth

Grind all ingredients and then blend and work into a putty-like mass, using rosewater or orange flower water. Moisten your hands with lavender oil, break off pieces of paste and roll into beads. Pierce with a needle for threading. Dry in a cool cupboard on greaseproof paper.

Herbs to Grow for Pot-pourri

The following are some of the many herbs suitable for pot-pourris.

angelica *(Angelica archangelica)*
bay or bay laurel *(Laurus nobilis)*

bergamot *(Monarda didyma)*
bluegum *(Eucalyptus globulus)*
borage *(Borago officinalis)*

box *(Buxus sempervirens)*
broom *(Sarothamus scoparius)*
calamint (mountain mint) *(Calamintha ascendens)*
calendula (English marigold) *(Calendula officinalis)*
camphor tree *(Cinnamomum camphora)*
caraway *(Carum carvi)*
carpet bugle *(Ajuga reptans)*
catmint or catnip *(Nepeta cataria, N. mussinii)*
chamomile *(Chamaemelum nobile)*
chicory *(Cichorium intybus)*
clary sage *(Salvia sclarea)*
clove carnation *(Dianthus caryophyllus)*
cockscomb *(Amaranth)*
columbine *(Aquilegia vulgaris)*
coriander *(Coriandrum sativum)*
cornflower *(Centaurea cyanus)*
costmary *(Chrysanthemum balsamita)*
cotton lavender *(Santolina chamaecyparissus)*
dandelion *(Taraxacum officinale)*
delphinium *(Delphinium grandiflorum, D. hybridum)*
dianthus – annual *(Dianthus allwoodii)*
dianthus – perennial *(Dianthus plumarius)*

dill *(Anethum graveolens)*

dog rose *(Rosa canina)*
eau-de-Cologne mint *(Mentha citrata)*
elder *(Sambucus nigra)*

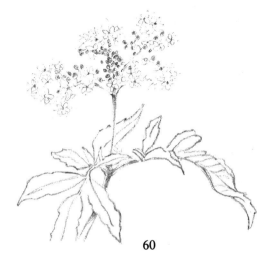

English lavender (*Lavandula angustifolia*)
fennel (*Foeniculum vulgare*)

fenugreek (*Trigonella foenum-graecum*)
feverfew (*Chrysanthemum parthenium*)
flax (*Linum usitatissimum*)
foxglove (*Digitalis purpurea*)
French lavender (*Lavandula dentata*)
garden valerian (*Centranthus ruber*)
gay feather (*Liatris pycnostachya*)
German chamomile (*Matricaria recutita*)
germander (*Teucrium chamaedrys*)
ginger (*Zingiber officinale*)

goldenrod (*Solidago virgaurea*)
ground ivy (*Glechoma hederacea*)
guelder rose (*Viburnum opulus*)
hawthorn (*Crataegus monogyna*)
heather (*Calluna vulgaris*)
hollyhock (*Althaea rosea*)
honeysuckle (*Lonicera caprifolium, L. periclymenum*)
hypericum (St John's wort) (*Hypericum perforatum*)
hyssop (*Hyssopus officinalis*)
iris – garden (*Iris versicolor*)
Jacob's ladder (*Polemonium caeruleum*)
Japanese rose (*Rosa rugosa*)
jasmine – yellow (*Gelsemium sempervirens*)
juniper (*Juniperis communis*)
larkspur (*Delphinium consolida*)
lavender – miniature (*Lavandula munstead*)
lemon balm (*Melissa officinalis*)

lemon thyme (*Thymus serpyllum*)

lemon tree (*Citrus limon*)
lemon verbena (citriodora) (*Aloysia triphylla*)
lily of the valley (*Convallaria majalis*)
lucerne (*Medicago sativa*)
mallow (common) (*Malva sylvestris*)
mimosa (*Acacia* species)
mints (*Mentha* species)
mullein (*Verbascum thapsus*)
myrtle (*Myrtus communis*)
nasturtium (*Tropaeolum majus*)
orange tree (*Citrus sinensis*)
oregano (*Origanum vulgare*)

ornamental opium poppy *(Papaver somniferum)*
orris *(Iris germanica)*
pansy *(Viola tricolor)*
pennyroyal *(Mentha pulegium)*
peony *(Paeonia officinalis)*
peppermint *(Mentha piperita)*
periwinkle *(Vinca major)*
pot marjoram *(Origanum onites)*
primrose *(Primula vulgaris)*
pyrethrum *(Chrysanthemum cinerariifolium)*
red clover *(Trifolium pratense)*
rose *(Rosa* varieties)
rosemary *(Rosmarinus officinalis)*

rue *(Ruta graveolens)*

sage *(Salvia officinalis)*
scented geranium *(Pelargonium graveolens)*
selfheal *(Prunella vulgaris)*
soapwort *(Saponaria officinalis)*
southernwood *(Artemisia abrotanum)*
Spanish lavender *(Lavandula stoechas)*

strawberry tree *(Arbutus unedo)*
summer savory *(Satureja hortensis)*
sunflower *(Helianthus annuus)*
sweet basil *(Ocimum basilicum)*
sweet briar *(Rosa eglanteria)*
sweet clover *(Melilotus alba)*
sweet marjoram *(Origanum majorana)*
sweet sedge *(Acorus calamus)*
tansy *(Tanacetum vulgare)*

tarragon *(Artemisia dracunculus)*

thyme – cooking *(Thymus vulgaris)*

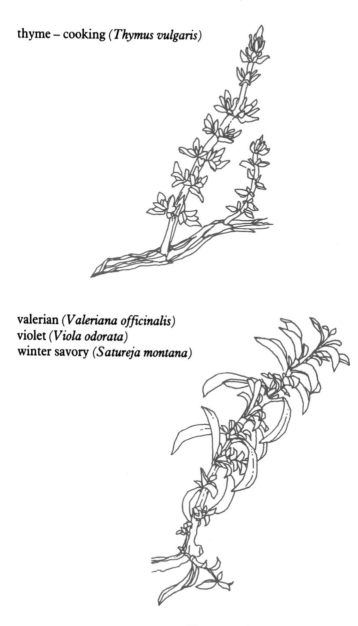

valerian *(Valeriana officinalis)*
violet *(Viola odorata)*
winter savory *(Satureja montana)*

woodruff *(Asperula odorata)*
wormwood *(Artemisia absinthium)*
yarrow *(Achillea millefolium)*

Trees to Grow for Pot-pourri

The flowers of the following trees can all be used for pot-pourri making.

African coral (*Erythrina caffra*)
almond (*Prunus amygdalus*)
bauhinia (*Bauhinia purpurea, B. blakeana*)
brush cherry (*Eugenia brasiliensis*)
Cape chestnut (*Calodendrum capense*)
Cape lilac (syringa) (*Melia azedarach*)
cherry (*Prunus* varieties)
firewheel tree (*Stenocarpus sinuatis*)
flamboyant (*Delonix regia*)
flowering gum – red (*Eucalyptus ficifolia*)
   (use leaves and seeds as well)
flowering peach (*Prunus persica*)
frangipani (*Plumeria rubra*)
gum – grey ornamental (*Eucalyptus pulverulenta*)
   (use leaves and seeds as well)
kapok tree (*Chorisia speciosa*)
mimosa (*Acacia floribunda*)
Monterey cypress (*Cupressus macrocarpa*)
peanut butter cassia (*Cassia didymobotrya*)
pink cassia (*Cassia javanica*)
pride of India (*Lagerstroemia indica*)
rose acacia (*Robinia hispida*)
rosewood (*Tipuana tipu*)
tibouchina (*Tibouchina granulosa*)
virgilia (*Virgilia oroboides*)

*Climbers to Grow
for Pot-pourri*

70

All of these climbers have the most beautiful flowers and all can be used in pot-pourri making. The plants are available at nurseries all over the country, and not only will they give much pleasure in the garden but they also make delightfully fragrant pot-pourri ingredients.

bignonia Mrs Rivers *(Distictis lactiflora)*
bougainvillea *(Bougainvillea* species)
clerodendrum *(Clerodendrum splendens)*
coral creeper *(Antigonon leptopus)*
dipladenia *(Mandavilla splendens)*
golden shower *(Pyrostegia venusta)*
granadilla – giant *(Passiflora quadrangularis)*
herald's trumpet creeper *(Beaumontia grandiflora)*
honeysuckle – common *(Lonicera periclymenum)*
honeysuckle – giant *(Lonicera hildebrandiana)*
jade vine *(Strongylodon macrobotrys)*
jasmine *(Jasminum polyanthum, J. stephanense)*
mandevilla *(Mandevilla laxa)*
petrea *(Petrea volubilis)*
potato creeper *(Solanum wendlandii)*
Rangoon creeper *(Quisqualis indica)*
stephanotis *(Stephanotis floribunda)*
thunbergia – blue *(Thunbergia grandiflora)*
travellers joy *(Clematis brachiata)*
trumpet bush *(Tecoma* varieties)
wisteria *(Wisteria sinensis)*

Shrubs to Grow for Pot-pourri

abelia (*Abelia chinensis*)
allamanda (*Allamanda cathartica*)
azalea (*Rhododendron indicum, R. molle*)
banksia (*Rosa banksia*)
barleria (*Barleria obtusa*)
bauhinia (*Bauhinia galpinii*)
bell heath (*Fabiana imbricata*)
bottlebrush (*Callistemon* varieties)
buddleia (*Buddleia salviifolia*)
carnival bush (*Ochna serrulata*)
cassia (*Cassia didymobotrya, C. multijuga*)
cestrum (*Cestrum willmottianum, C. purpureum*)
Chinese hydrangea (*Hydrangea macrophylla*)
Chinese lantern (*Abutilon hybridum*)
clerodendrum (*Clerodendrum fragrans, C. foetidum*)

dombeya (*Dombeya dregeana*)
duranta (*Duranta repens*)
elder (*Sambucus nigra*)
eucalyptus – ornamental (*Eucalyptus rhondantha*)
forsythia (*Forsythia intermedia*)
gardenia (*Gardenia thunbergia, G. jasminoides*)
heather (*Erica* species)
honeysuckle (*Loncera* varieties)
jasmine (*Jasminum officinale, J. revolutum*)
Jerusalem sage (*Phlomis fruticosa*)
jungle flower (*Chrysanthemoides monilifera*)
lavender (*Lavandula spica, L. dentata*)
lemon verbena (*Aloysia citriodora* or *Lippia citriodora*)
lion's tail (*Leonotis leonurus*)
mace shrub (*Calycanthus floridus*)

malaleuca (*Melaleuca nesophylla*)
may (*Spiraea arguta, S. cantoniensis*)
mock orange (*Philadelphus coronarius*)
myrtle (*Myrtus communis, M. ugni*)

Natal plum (*Carissa grandiflora*)
orange jessamine (*Murraya exotica*)
petrea (*Petrea volubilis*)
plectranthus (*Plectranthus fruticosus*)
plumbago (*Plumbago auriculata*)
pompom bush (*Pimelea rosea*)
pride of Barbados (*Caesalpinia pulcherrima*)
rock rose (*Cistus villosus*)
rose (*Rosa* varieties)
Turk's cap (*Malvaviscus mollis*)
snowball flower (*Viburnum opulus*)
Spanish broom (*Spartium junceum*)
tassel flower (*Calliandra brevipes*)
tamarix (*Tamarix aphylla*)
tecoma (*Tecoma* varieties)
tibouchina (*Tibouchina elegans*)
wild lilac (*Buddleia asiatica*)
yesterday, today and tomorrow (*Brunfelsia pauciflora*)
yucca (*Yucca filamentosa*)

Glossary of Terms

You may find that many pot-pourri recipes include names in their lists of ingredients which may be confusing or unfamiliar to the pot-pourri maker. This glossary should help to clarify this problem. Many ingredients can be ordered from a chemist or importer.

Acacia   Gum acacia or gum arabic. A type of resin, used in the making of pomanders and scented beads. It has nothing to do with our acacia trees.

Ambergris   A substance formed in the intestinal tract of the sperm whale. It has great fixative powers, and a rich and fascinating odour. It is still used in perfumery today in spite of the whale becoming an endangered species.

Balm   Lemon balm or *Melissa officinalis*. A lemon flavoured and scented herb much loved in pot-pourris.

Balm of Gilead   A small tree *(Populus candicans)*, native to Saudi Arabia. The buds have a rich balsamic fragrance which is long lasting in pot-pourri.

Balsam of Peru (Myroxylon pereirae)   A fragrant black resin, obtained by heating and beating the bark of this tree, which is native to Central America. The oil is used in pot-pourris and medicine.

Bay salt   Sea salt.

Benzoin   A fragrant resin obtained from Styrax trees which are grown in Sumatra and Thailand. Used in perfumery as a fixative. Also known as *Gum benzoin, Benjamin styrax, Storax, Oil of Ben.*

Bergamot (Monarda didyma)   Richly aromatic, bergamot oil is a unique citrus oil obtained from the orange *(Citrus bergamia)* grown in southern Italy. It is used to give Earl Grey tea its distinctive aroma and flavour. Used sparingly, the oil is a

75

superb pot-pourri ingredient. Also known as *Bee balm* or *Oswega*.

Borax   A chemical substance, *Sodium borate*, used in the manufacture of glass and ceramics; it is also a cleansing agent. Combined with salt, it keeps pot-pourri fresh. It can also be used in the drying of flowers by covering each flower with borax until dry.

Calamint (Calamintha officinalis)   A small bushy herb with fragrant downy leaves that have a camphorous odour. It is moth repellent, and difficult to grow successfully.

Calamus (Acorus calamus)   The ground and powdered rhizome is used as a fixative. Belonging to the arum lily family, it is sweet smelling and easy to grow. It likes moist and shady places. Also known as *Sweet flag, Sedge, Bog iris, Sweet rush, Sweet iris*.

Cascarilla   Aromatic bark of the *Croton eluteria*, a close relative of the castor oil tree; native to Honduras. Once used in incense and in fumigating blocks or pastilles. Has a strong fragrance.

Cassia (Cinnamomum cassia)   A tree grown in Ceylon. Chips or small pieces of bark are used in pot-pourri. Also known as *Chinese cinnamon*.

Cedarwood   The evergreen coniferous tree of the genus *Cedrus*. Used either as an oil or as chips of wood. Moth repellent, and has a strong, pungent fragrance that is very long lasting.

Clary (Salvia sclarea)   Leaves are used as a fixative. It can be grown in the garden as a biennial, and all parts of the plant are used in pot-pourri. Also known as *Clary sage* or *Giant sage*.

Clove pink (Dianthus caryophyllus)   Old-fashioned pink or carnation dianthus from the wide variety of the carnation family. Has a distinct clove-like perfume and is excellent in pot-pourris. Also known as *Gillyflower* or *Clove dianthus*.

Costmary (Tanacetum balsamita)   Once used as a stewing herb, its fragrant, balsam-like leaves are much prized in pot-pourris.

Cotton lavender (Santolina incana)   A bushy, green-leaved, pungent smelling herb, with brilliant yellow button flowers, well known in South Africa. As an insect-repelling herb, santolina is useful in pot-pourris.

Cubebs (Piper cubeba)   A climbing vine or shrub, native to Indonesia and Java, which produces berries in midsummer. The berries resemble peppercorns and their fragrance is hot and spicy. Also used in condiments.

Cypress or Cypres (Cupressus sempervirens)   A coniferous, evergreen and fragrant tree native to western Asia. Leaves and small cones used in pot-pourri.

Dittany (Dictamnus albus)   A small shrub with intensely fragrant leaves. Dittany of Crete is no relation. Also known as *Burning bush.*

Elderflower (Sambucus nigra)   Flowers used in pot-pourri. They have a vanilla-like scent and dry quickly. Also known as *Elderberry* or *Elder.*

Frankincense   A fragrant gum or resin that oozes from the wounded bark of this forest tree, *Boswellia thunifera*, which is native to Saudi Arabia. Main ingredient in Church incense and used as a fixative in pot-pourri. Also known as *Olibanum.*

Fumitory (Adlumia fungosa)   A close relative of the poppy and native to England, the petals are used in wash-balls and in pot-pourri.

Ground ivy (Glechoma hederacea)   An ubiquitous creeping indoor and hothouse plant with fragrant, heart-shaped leaves. Leaves used in pot-pourri. The long trailing stems make it a beautiful hanging-basket plant.

Gum tragacanth   A resin or mucilage made from the tree *Astragalus gummifer,* and mixed with water (usually ½ tsp gum to ½ cup water) makes a gluey substance. Used in cake decorating and pot-pourri pastilles.

Garde-robe (Artemisia abrotanum)   Its French name indicates that this herb was used to keep clothes free from moths. Its insecticide properties are well known and its function as an ingredient in pot-pourris is to keep insects away. Also known as *Southernwood* or *Lad's love*.

Helichrysum (Helichrysum angustifolium)   A wide range of 'straw flowers' or everlastings. Used not for their perfume but for their colour and shape appeal in an open bowl of pot-pourri. Some have a curry-like smell that can predominate, so be careful how you use them.

Hyssop (Hyssopus officinalis)   Dried leaves and flowers make an interesting addition to pot-pourri. It is the source of a valuable essential oil.

Jasmine (Jasminum officinale)   Native to India, the climbing flowers of jasmine varieties, and the indigenous South African ones, are all exquisite in pot-pourri. Also known as *Jessamine*.

Juniper berries (Juniperus communis)   The dried aromatic berries and prickly leaves can be added to pot-pourri, crushing the berries first. Oil is also extracted from the berries.

Khus-khus   An aromatic grass from the West Indies used as a fixative. The dried root has a long-lasting aroma similar to sandalwood and myrrh. Can be grown successfully in most places. Also known as *Vetiver*.

Labdanum (Cistus incanus)   This fragrant, very bitter resin comes from the leaves of the Cretan rock rose. Used as a fixative.

Lilac (Syringa vulgaris)   With its sweet-smelling mauve or white clusters of flowers, lilac is a well-known garden shrub which originated in Persia and was introduced into England in the sixteenth century.

Linden (Tilia cordata)   The flowers are sometimes included in pot-pourri recipes. They are the sweet-smelling, lime-green flowers of the lime trees indigenous to Europe.

Mace   The outer covering or membrane of the nutmeg, *Myristica fragrans*, native to the Molucca Islands. Added to pot-pourri it is a fixative.

Magalep (Prunus mahaleb)   Native to central and southern Europe, the berries or kernels of this type of wild cherry are used in pot-pourris. They can also be threaded to make fragrant bracelets or necklaces.

Marsh mallow (Althaea officinalis)   The flowers are used in pot-pourris and, although indigenous to Europe and Britain, it can be grown in most places.

Mastic (Pistacia lentiscus)   A clear gum resin made by wounding the bark of the Lentisc tree. Indigenous to the Mediterranean, it is cultivated for its gum on the island of Chios. Used in the manufacture of Turkish delight, dental adhesives and varnishes, it is also an ingredient in incense and pomanders. Also known as *Mastich*.

Musk   The oil obtained from the musk glands located between the anus and sexual organs of the musk deer have led to the near extinction of this animal. Fortunately, oil of musk is now manufactured synthetically. Plants such as the moss rose, hyacinth and angelica have a musk fragrance and they can be used in pot-pourris.

Myrrh (Commiphora myrrha)   A precious resin obtained from a tree native to Saudi Arabia. This aromatic oleo-resin has been used for thousands of years in perfumery, incense and embalming.

Neroli   The oil extracted from the bitter orange. It was said to have originated in Italy. It is also used in perfumery.

Oak moss   A lichen that grows on oak trees and has a distinctive aroma. Used as a fixative, it also forms the base of the Chypre-type perfume.

Oil of spike   A fragrant oil with a very strong aroma, distilled from a species of lavender *(Lavandula spica)*. It is much used in perfumery and can be used as an oil in pot-pourris. It is also used as an artist's oil paint medium.

Opoponax (Commiphora myrrha)   An exudation from the Commiphora tree – from which myrrh is obtained. Oil of opoponax can be bought and it has a strong oriental fragrance. Used as a fixative.

Orris (Iris florentina)   The powdered, dried rhizome of this specific iris and perhaps the best known of all fixatives. It smells like violets, and is indigenous to the Mediterranean region. Its flowers are palest mauve or white and not particularly attractive.

Patchouli (Pogostemon patchouli) A haunting oil, powerfully strong, distilled from the leaves of the patchouli plant. It is a member of the mint family, native to Penang, Malaysia and Paraguay. It is used to scent saris and woven shawls, and as a moth repellent. It should be used with utmost care.

Petitgrain oil This oil is the extract from the skin of the bitter orange and is used in perfumery.

Rhodium (Lignum rhodium) The wood cut from the underground roots of *Convolvulus floridus* and *Convolvulus scopatius*, indigenous to the Canary Islands. The sweet-scented oil distilled from the woody roots is greatly prized in perfumery and in pot-pourris.

Sandalwood (Santalum album) Indigenous to Asia, this is a favourite fragrance, and rasping and chips are available. Oil of sandalwood in synthetic form is pleasant, and chips and oils are important fixatives. Also known as *Santal*, *Sanders*, or *Santalum*.

Sassafras (Sassafras officinalis) Native to North America, chips from the root and bark make an interesting addition to pot-pourris.

Spikenard (Nardostachys jatamansi) An aromatic fibrous root from a dwarf shrub native to the Himalayas. Still used today in China as an ingredient in fragrant baths. Not to be confused with a British herb, Ploughman's spikenard (*Inula conyza*). Spikenard is a rich oil popular as a perfume in the East, but is replaced by oil of valerian in modern perfumery.

Storax (Styrax) A treacle-like gum with an agreeable, musky odour that is extracted by pressing the bark of the liquid amber tree. Indigenous to the island of Rhodes and parts of Asia Minor. The gum is used as a fixative.

Tonka or *Tonquin beans (Dipteryx odorata)* The black fragrant, almond-shaped seed of a large South American tree. It is used as a fixative, as well as in scenting pipe tobacco, and as an ingredient in perfumes.

Notes

Notes

Notes

Notes

Notes

Notes

Notes